LIKE ME

Contents

I

II

III

EPILOGUE

I.

PLUNGE YOUR ARM IN UP TO THE ELBOW

The ocean receded. I watch myself in the mirror. *From the city,*
head north the directions say.

I sit on the bed in my bright green T-shirt and white shorts. My
face, the smooth tan of foundation. I am constructed. Everything
around me is green. X-rayed, baked, photographed with

special equipment. Let me tell you, nobody likes me. It matches
my eyes.

I watch myself in the mirror. My shirt falls squarely. Stamen flush
with light. My thighs spread against the quilt. I have a body. This
sets the tourist in motion.

On the day the last stone house is built, I build myself in the
mirror. Follow directions. I do

the cover-up. It holds me. I do the hairspray. The suck-in. I about-
face. I am lonely. At one regional opening continue straight into
one day she says *you'll learn to like yourself.*

PLUNGE YOUR ARM IN UP TO THE ELBOW

At the other regional opening, admire a flute of white moths.

I am still watching myself in the mirror. At its most bulbous, we are at dance class. I watch myself in the mirror and feel sick. X-rayed, baked, photographed with special equipment.

The fluorescent light rains down hard. *Turn L off the highway into the mirror.* I am framed by. X-rayed, baked. At its most bulbous, I am alone in the gaze. Inside the studio, the sky is low

with the breath of jealous girls. I am still building what will hold me. I am that breadth. In the mirror I stagger after. Somewhere there's an insides. My body a flabby container. It is time

to feel something. But it cannot match my face. In the mirror I set the tourist in motion. Like a funhouse the shape wavers. See how it becomes me. I draw an X in the steam of breath

on the mirror. It is time to close the gateway of the ribs or spill out. It's my turn to cross the floor.

We put water balloons down our bathing suit tops that summer and

posed for pictures. After driving 92.3 miles all I see is her beauty.

As one blunt thing I have no body. I must separate into parts.

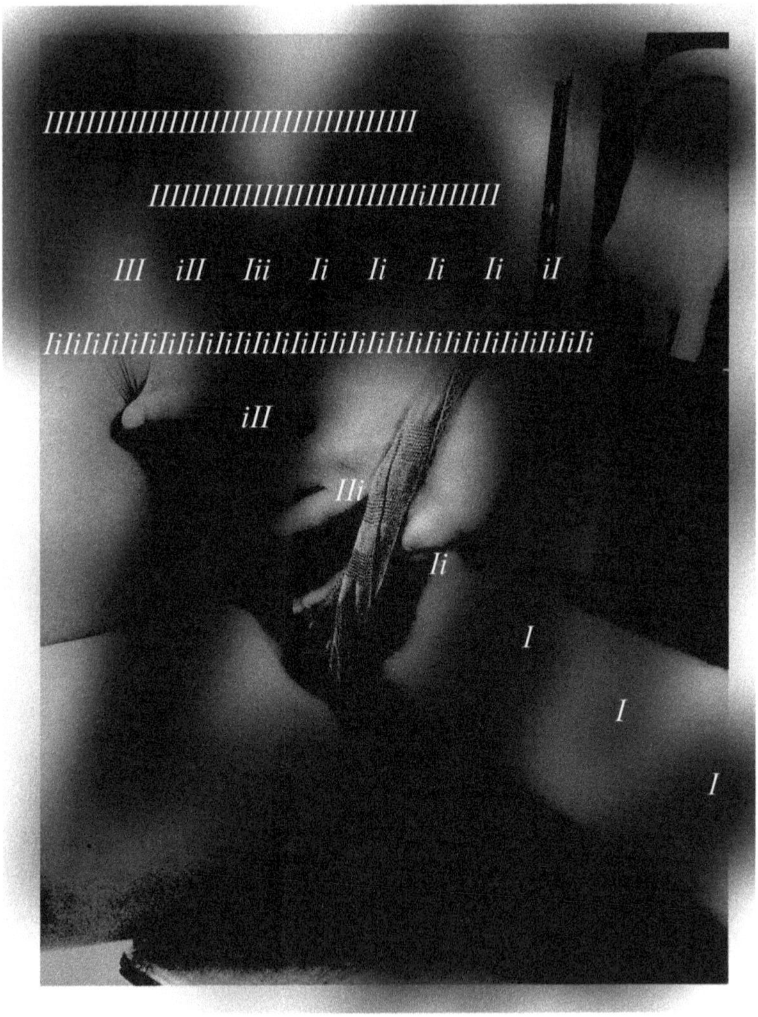

TO BE OR like NOT TO BE

The ocean receded. I sit on the bleachers in my cotton gym shorts.
Over the blunt ends of my knees, I watch her fight back. Rites of
passage. She throws the basketball *like* right in Natalie's

face.

Her black hair like two curtains ripped open. Black widow's peak,
her mouth ringed orange like fun. The spit of cover-up parts her
witch hair. What surprise lights up her wicked white girl face.

What wicked white girl face of my dreams. The gymnasium floor
shrieks. I watch her *like* claw out. *Out* out. Girl pieces whir. Her
fingers in motion. Aware the pronoun's confusing. It's true

they pull hair. I am not *like* a fighter, but you have to kill the pretty
girl. Middle school queen. You have to dig in with your body. I
watch. See my fingers curl. I watch them get physical.

Right through the make-up. Right through our wicked white scene.
Heat bloods to the surface and mingles. Another *like* sistering.
Silver hoops hook and tear. What I wouldn't give to dig in.

See the red smear pop on the lacquered floor. Where the sun hits it's blinding. I squint over the blunt end of my knees. All I want is a body. To rip into. Not my own. Not my own legs.

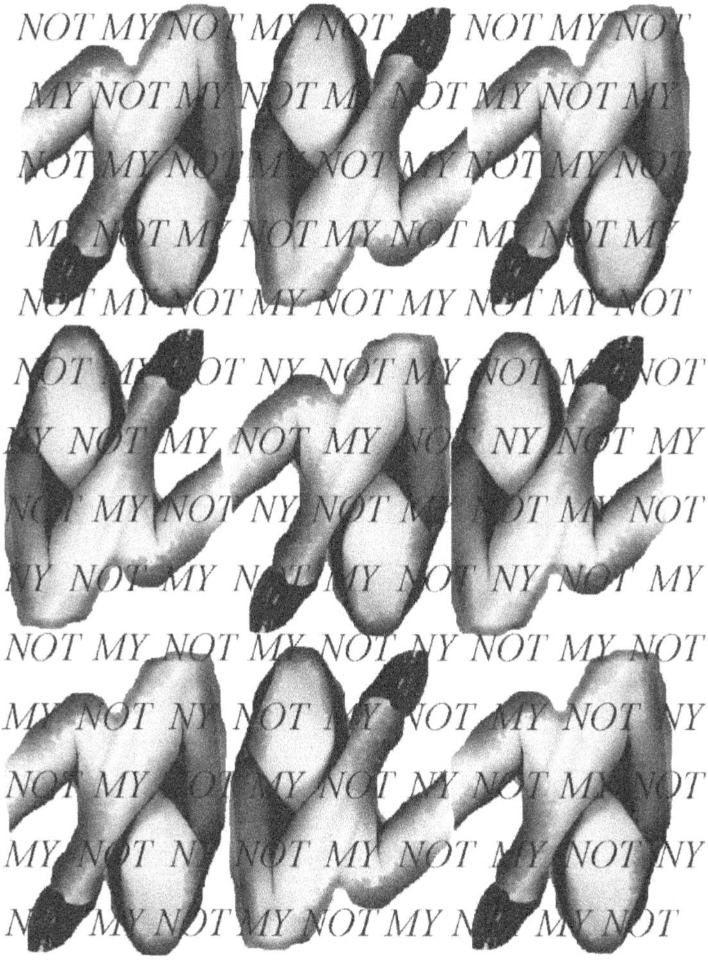
NOT MY

TO BE OR like NOT TO BE

The ocean receded. I puff around the oval track. Gravel nips

my shins. *Say your name and a verb that begins with the same letter.*

Do the motion. I puff around the oval track. I grasp the stick in

one hand. *J is for... J is for...* I watch her silver hoop earrings, her

bright blond hair. See me follow. See her blond hair bounce, tail of her

white polo fluttering. See me follow. My breath *like*

burns. We each see the ball, grasp our stick, hooked and handled.

See her sprint down the field. Her lips curl back, see two eyeteeth

even whiter than pearl. See her verb things. *S is for sinuous*

S is for supple S is for sex

-y. She holds the field hockey stick across her hips in two fists.

Miss Piggy Miss Piggy she sings. The stick hooked and handled. *J*

is for... She pugs her nose with one finger and laughs. See

my own fingers curl.

PLUNGE YOUR ARM IN UP TO THE ELBOW

I watch the pretty girls roll up their tights. Leg by leg. I scratch my
white thigh. I must have something. I pull up my hem. Feet slap
the blond boards. I tug and I tug and I tug. This sets the tourist in

motion.

How to posture elsewhere. Map out the roads to her cave. To make
her cloud animals dance at a look. I hold the red-brown smears to
my nose and inhale. It is not the same as your blood. Here

is where the forest will part. I am hoarding secrets off the map. To
make her lakes gleam blue. To gleam blue in reflection. No one
would step off the path if there's path. Tell me your lies.

I peer out between the leaves of my anger. They match my green
eyes. The girls are dancing the path, their pale pink tights trace a
longing. A flutter like wings in the dust. If you look in my eyes

you can see the reflection. This sets the tourist in motion.

That summer a boy puts his hands down my pants. It hurts.

Over and over. My toes bloody from dancing. I tug and I tug and I tug.

The truth is, I like a little pain. That summer I buy my first skirt.

TO BE OR like NOT TO BE

The ocean receded. I fold the paper in a neat rectangle. It pulls

open with one tab. I watch my hand make an arrow. In the cave of

tween sorrows, it takes *like* whole minutes for your eyes to

adjust. Each place where we touch. I scratch out our joints with my

pen. Scratch matching leggings. Scratch sleepover sundaes.

Scratch tampon lessons in the closet. Scratch her father's

loud laughter, her father's big hands. It's *like* time to start over.

There is a path in the woods and

I am adjusting. See the landmarks red with desire. Blue ink

showing through where I wrote her. All the nasty things. It takes

whole minutes. And where is the lie?

Yes   *No*   *Maybe*

Time to mark her 'til the pen tears the page. I watch my hand place the note in his locker. My hand makes an arrow. I am *like* learning a lesson. The blue ink shows right through our skin.

PLUNGE YOUR ARM IN UP TO THE ELBOW

I watch myself in the mirror. I watch myself in the mirror for days.
Her face hardens where I learn to adjust. Look I've made pieces. I
wipe my hands on the bed. I stick my fingers in my

cunt. I can't stop selecting. My body right from the mirror. Out
here it spreads green and dirty. I would like to fold into. Fold her
into my body. Nude crayon color ecstasy. I would airy and light.

Or clear as glass with nothing reflecting. There is hope for me yet.
But before I pave over, I dig with my fingers. I dig for my heart.

We all have four limbs, they say. A skin

White as paper White as snow White as milk White as salt White as a statue White as a diamond White as sunbeams White as sea foam White as white satin White as camphor White as silver White as alabaster White as arsenic White as morning White as moonshine White as frost White as ivory White as porcelain White as soap White as a moonlit sail White as a flashing icicle White as the necks of swans White as a swan's stray feather White as some baby's arm White as a flock of sheep White as a single sheep White as a sin forgiven White as a sycamore White as a whale's tooth White as a bear's tooth White as chastity White as gulls White as the breast of a gull White as the blossoms of the almond tree White as the foam that danced on the billow's height White as the hand of Moses White like the egg of the pigeon hen White as wax White as a curd White as the winding-sheet White as death White as fleece White as death White as molten glass White as truth White as a chicken White as a bridal veil White as an angel White as a ceiling White as a coif White as a school boy's paper kite White as sea fog White as thistle-down White as a dove White as a lily White as the gleam of her beckoning hand White as flame White as bone White as a flock of egrets White as steel in a furnace White like a daisy in a field of grass White as a pillow White as a sheet White as the apparition of a rainbow White as faith's and age's hue White as ashes White as grit White as a custard White as sugar White as a fish White as a doll White as a ghost White as charnel bone White as cold boil'd veal and

White as appetite. Bold as blank page. A blank page, they say. And an insides. I put my heart in my mouth and smile. I smile without showing my teeth.

[THIS PAGE INTENTIONALLY LEFT BLANK]

PLUNGE YOUR ARM IN UP TO THE ELBOW

I started masturbating at a young age. Without pleasure for the
body, pleasure in the body. Otherwise known as the scientific
method. I watch myself in the mirror. Her skin holds

my face. I prayer my hands and mount them. The rise of certain
landmarks. I watch myself in silence, one cheek pressed to the
sheets. Everything around me is green. Then

it explodes.

I tell myself pretty. *Here* and *here* with the blade of my hands. I
could look in the mirror for hours. Rise and dip of certain
landmarks. So you know where to turn. I turn my heart

over with my tongue. I tell myself pretty. This is a story for
tourists. *Here* and *here* I open my legs. Sometimes the breadth of a
pillow, corner of the mattress, the cold wooden floor. It

wasn't until later I needed to put something inside me.

qp

db

TO BE OR like NOT TO BE

The ocean receded. All my dreams went dark. In the sealed cave of
my insides see the spotlight strike Sheri's hair. Now I am coming.
Field hockey stick, hooked and handled. I practice. I press

my fat unto glass. Unto

screen unto windowpane. See the pretty girls wick into. It's *like*
cool to the touch. I *like* practice. To make the balls crack. I circle
the parts on my body. Sometimes with resin, sometimes

with neon, sometimes with teeth. Field hockey stick weighted, wed
for two fists. I press my fat unto. *Miss Piggy Miss Piggy.* Clumps
of blond hair. I present the stick in my fists. You have to

kill the pretty girl. So *duh*   I practice my stroke. Feel the
vibrations deep in my throat:

Yes   *No*   *Maybe*

Feel her cheekbones crack into place. Her ribs latch unto. Getting hard in the glass. I've got *like* a new room inside me. Her laughter bubbles red in my throat. I wipe the stick clean on her skirt.

II.

CONTINUOUS FAMILY OWNERSHIP

The ocean receded. There is the mother. Once upon a time, it was
her first and only divorce. But is that a beginning? Then she lost
her father. Once upon a time, she had no more men.

There is the daughter. Someone walking in a circle. There is the
mother, and there the daughter. Outside the snow a stilling blanket.
Inside the girl shape doubles around our hands. We make

donuts from my great-grandmother's recipe. She feeds me three
generations. She feeds me butter and whole milk and cream. She is
happy until the mirror cracks. She is happy until she isn't

and I'll never understand. She says *mirror mirror*. She says *I was
no great beauty*. She chips the pink tile from the bathroom walls. I
think of it like *my grandmother is coming, my grandmother*

is coming! My mother says she was clothed and fed but that's
where her mother's love ends. Still grandma comes through her.
See, there's an insides. Edges sharpened to a bitter blue keen.

In my princess dream, the snow covers her tracks and the deer

make new ones. Dinner is lovely, the garden is lovely. In reality

I'm not sure these are my hands. *I am no great beauty* says my

mother and sets the table for two. *Only daughter.* I grasp the hem

of her skirt. I chew out a hole. She talks for hours at the table. I

leave slices of bread in the basket. I learn how to run. *Mommy,*

I'm sorry, I can't make you become. Now. The clear blue anger. I

am going, I should not be going, I should never go, I best go *now.*

She wants someone to open her. Thinks she's vessel, needs an

anchor, wants to see herself make a shape in his hands. My father

tells me I have beautiful eyes. I eat with my hands. Lick my

fingers. Even without men there are men. Mommy never touched

me, but when the dishes are dirtied there's only me and her left to

blame. Even without men there is violence. I'll eat chicken over

and over and like it. I'll sleep and sleep until noon. *Mirror*

mirror. Her face shuts down like a spoon. There is my

grandmother's china. Her color a bitter blue keen. Once I had a mother. Someone walking in a circle. A heap of pink tile in the

sun. I

turn off the path into shadow, put out my hands. Let me tell you
what, literally. *I am no great beauty* says my mother. The thing is
she won't ever just punish me. This is my story and you're *not*

even listening. Her face is the first mirror I see.

WHILE THE ORIGINS OF THE TERM REMAIN OBSCURE

The ocean receded. We are at the mall. I have decided everything

makes me look fat. What *I* that I'm given. She has those breasts,

nude and wireless. *Dear Mommy, you do know I'm not your*

man. She makes a pained face. I say *I'm just fat. It's all fat.* A

well-lit stage. What is a daughter? I gnaw a nub of affection. A

forever companion without her own means. Hide beneath

the round clothing racks. The carpet rough on my knees. The

mirror reassembles. It's my turn to do up her pearlized buttons. My

turn to fashion, my turn to step into the pain. This is a pain

you have chosen and I'll choose it again. Like childbirth it is

coming from in you. Remember,

there is some ritual. I watch her mouth, a little crooked in the

mirror. *Mirror mirror.* I must clip myself into the body like

mommy. Dear Mommy. *I am no great beauty.*

This is all just what I've been told.

She takes me to the reservoir. In her string bikini and lotion, me a softly-furred animal toeing the sand. Mommy laid out on wooden slats. I swim 'til my ears scream.

CONTINUOUS FAMILY OWNERSHIP

The ocean receded. In the dream she surfaces inside my childhood

friend. Says *I only wanted a daughter, I couldn't even name you.*

Husband and lover right under little mother. The cherry

my cherry, my mouth Mommy mouth. The lock on my bedroom

door. You have to kill the pretty girl. Her mouth come fragile.

Singing about edible flowers. *You must make blood to woman*

is something he told me. *The choice is in you, just open your legs.* I

pluck a broken piece of pink tile from the heap and turn it in my

hand. Here is my mother's work. The obvious step is to build

something. I hold the jagged edge to my skin. It is time to cut out a

feature, but I need a schematic, a diagram. The only map is for

tourists. The blood is all wrong, like smeared paste

in my panties. I'm still sitting on the toilet when my grandmother

slaps me *for good luck.*

WHILE THE ORIGINS OF THE TERM REMAIN OBSCURE

The ocean receded. The dressing room at Contempo Casuals has
no doors and two wall-length mirrors. From my corner it spreads
out like the maze in a royal garden. The green carpeted path

wends through white shrubbery. All the angles are open. From my
cornerest corner I do not want her to see me undressed. White
walls mark her parts on my body. I pluck the gaze 'til each part

vibrates as one. My skin prickles. I smooth the white mohair
sweater over my breasts. Here are my breasts. The gaze undoes
into parts. This is the midriff reclamation act. All her bodies in the

room nearly naked for combat. *I am no great beauty.* I creep out in
the mirror. All her bodies reproduce walls. Mother brandishes the
color wheel. A bloody bout of compliments. She says *yes.* She says

no. She says *yes.* Aware the pronoun is confusing. Later she burns
her knees on the carpeted floor of his car, face in his lap. Her
weight in my hands.

CONTINUOUS FAMILY OWNERSHIP

Then comes the part where I am the best. I am the best ever. The

backbone stupid. So there was a goat could speak as if trolls and a

water under the bridge. There's my girl in the box

'neath the second pine. Clouds part. I hurt people on purpose. This

is what I learned from my mom. A gold dirt. Sit me down to

whisky every night. I am exactly as dirty as I dream.

So I inherited my grandmother's heels, her lamb's wool coat, and

her penchant for fashion over fit. *Mommy, this is how you die.*

Through the brown water, brown fish like children dream.

I was daughter, then I had to be her everything. I was *like* the dog

and *like* I was her husband and *like* whatever else. It's not fair, but

I'm not a fair person. Later she tells me I was terrible to live with

in high school. That's *codependence* my friend says. That's *an only*

daughter growing up with a single mother I reply.

WHILE THE ORIGINS OF THE TERM REMAIN OBSCURE

We are at the mall. A well-lit stage. History pivots on the moment

this would look cuter on you

CONTINUOUS FAMILY OWNERSHIP

The ocean receded. My mother drives us over the mountain in
silence. We slide between trees. Carried in anger by her own
silence. Obtruding classical music and I know it's my fault.

Here, where the moon opens the black valley with silver. Here,
where the trees close like lacing overhead. From generation to
generation. The windows vibrate with anger. I never know what's

my fault. The little lights on the dashboard flare and dim with her
surge. I finger my silver rings. Here, where the trees close overhead.
Not the sharp kind of tool, a conductor. Note

the silence. The dark sweep and dizzying lift of night sky above
the valley, where black is the beginning of space. In the daughter
box, I hold shape. She turns the wheel. Now comes the long

stretch between trees. Out of the silence, a violin moans. Out of
silence all the things you can never take back. Here where the
headlights pick out each tree trunk, the black lace of spruce. My

mouth sour meat. I imagine a cave in the woods. A small fire, a

pile of furs. Even daughters are handy. I know I can skin a rabbit. I

know how to fashion a trap.

DESIGNATION AS NATIONAL HISTORIC LANDMARK

It is hot inside the car. I sweat into the armpits of my new jacket.

History *like* pivots on the moment

CONTINUOUS FAMILY OWNERSHIP

My mother and I head homeward. Here is where the trees close
like lacing and the road turns like a hook. We are each singing a
song from our own generation. Moving in tandem like oxen

yoked.

An obsession with the rearview. Linda Ronstadt, Bonnie Raitt, Joni
Mitchell, Carol King. I press my hand to the window. It leaves a
mark. I spill a little through the cool glass. Eyes dark up

with night, skin smoothed with shadow. The mark turns and I turn.
I fix my gaze on the mark. We plow headlong into her double
reflection. Darkness exchanged for darkness. Hand of my

hand. I spill a little out the mark. The generation slips sideways.
Anger must flow in one direction. The generation slips sideways
and I upset the balance. Here comes the hairpin turn.

III.

THE CORN OR THE like STORY OF THE CORN

The ocean receded. I watch his hands on my body. My black lace

bra, hip-slung jeans. Smell bread baking. Caramel crusted cider.

He stands behind me in the mirror. Smell the light rotting

quietly, powdering of mold. *Look how good we look* I say. I am

looking at my body. I make *like* a shape in his hands. Where my

hips flare. His fingers are long and rounded. I watch his fingers

on my body. Light rotting quietly. He and I are good friends. I put

my hands over his. I spread our fingers all through us. I fill my body

in his hands. It's *like...* It's *like...* *Like* it's grown all through

us. Watch my shape in the mirror. Down by the secret swimming

hole. Down by the riverbend. On the flood plains along the route to

the Mountain House. Watch it *like* spread. Smell the light rotting,

alien bloom of mold. *If you can see it* they say *don't cut it out.* It's

like already through everything.

Explore! Enjoy!

Discover!

Unspoiled!
Secluded!

Unspoiled! Beauty!

THE WORD GIRLFRIEND

The ocean receded. I have a boy and we are in love. It is easy this
way. I watch from the corduroy nest of the armchair. Tara smokes
epically. I still look clumsy with cigarettes. I draw my knees

up over my body. I draw less. Still life with *who doesn't want to be
cool.* I watch her mouth now. Her voice is *like* right out of *Daria.* I
smoke his cigarette. I watch my mouth. Where

the hard girl shell slits open. Watch what comes out. *That slut.* It
comes out of my throat all *like* fortified by centuries. I plug my
mouth with cigarette. I swallow what comes out. Here and there

I bristle through. Filigree of stalks. It's *like* time for a change.
Fingers to my lips, I inhale. New eyes, all blind. His body a screen
where we each have an entry. *That slut.*

I have *like* so much to learn.

THE CORN OR THE like STORY OF THE CORN

When I dial the phone rings and rings. When I wait it won't speak.

It is time to wait. There is no mirror without my face. The loose

folds of velvet pet my legs. The animal inside is hot, it's *like*

hungry. I feed it cookies and cranberry juice. My own fingers. I've

spent whole summers without friends. In the pages of books I press

my body to so many worlds. This time the animal's still

cagey. It wants flesh. Boundaries of skin it can chew through. It

wants to make shape. In the story possibilities proliferate. *Mirror*

mirror. I will always be ugly. Animal sees with my eyes, it feels

with my breath, it *like* tears its own hair a little. What else is all

through me? I take my clothes off in front of the mirror. Push my

breasts up in my hands. Pigeon-toe. Lift out of the crown

of my head. Animal turns the crown into bedding. It makes and

unmakes. I'm not *like* saying this is more natural. The eye of the

camera clicks with my blink, the screen is an entry.

Animal's not angry. If the tools are claws, clicks, or pages. If the tools are his hands. The phone's really not helping. I love my own company, but if I keep nibbling my insides I'll *like* never fill out.

The sun shines yellow, unmoved. I could just close the pages and go for a walk. After heroes and magpies. After iced tea and crinolines. After crocuses, daffodils, *like* roses, linoleum. There's

a slab of rock on the mountain, warm even under the stars. I don't count them. In my body the phone rings and rings.

THE WORD GIRLFRIEND

Or sit me alone on a page. And *like* what of her taken up with a
straw. I inhale. Light a cigarette. This is a boring story. Everyone
knows how it ends. So I draw in a spaceship. I draw in a tail and

like fangs. I draw the word out of my body. Not through the mouth.
Turn up the heat lamp, turn up her heroine eyes. Time flows and
eddies. I watch her on the busted orange couch. I am *like*

my whole body. Mouth shut, I smoke the word out. It comes off
me in waves. But now what. I lean toward her, she draws it out like
metal filings. A string of paper dolls. She's this magnet but

what am I. *That what. What*

what. He vibrates between. I lick the salt edge of my thumb. I
finally have a boy here. The difficulty is figuring out where to get
off. The art of ringing all your bells.

Later, I lick her off his teeth. And during all of it, the river ran

north.

THE WORD GIRLFRIEND

The ocean receded. I watch them make out in the hall outside the cafeteria door. There I am in my metal choker, plaid skirt, and black boots, talking to my friend. But I am watching them

make out. They are the new girls. She with blue hair all *like* matching her eyes. She in the velvet tank top. With beautiful tits. I feel my face flake.   I am all eyes.

My friend's words slow to moan. The hall fills with smoke. I'm *like* so dramatic. The girl husk flakes away and I can barely lick it together. Quick to cocoon, slow to *like* change. I am all eyes. *Like*

a filigree of stalks. I watch myself watching. This is *like* ah

ah

ah

AAAA

An abundance of silver rings. I get feelings. An abundance. A *like*
abundance of

E

NTE

R

THE

FIR

ST

REA

LIZ

ATI

ON

THE CORN OR THE like STORY OF THE CORN

Tumbled on the comforter and I am some shape, all tumbled, all

ready to fill up on his hands. Smell the light rotting quietly. In the

field, in our beds. Someone owns all of it. The phone is ringing.

And ringing. He and I, we show up late to the study session and

like everyone knows. Later she's all like *don't invite her to your*

birthday. The sun shines blankly. He apologizes

on the phone. I watch my body in the mirror. Time again to trim

the *like* bad parts. Picked, plucked, and powdered. Shucked our

clothes and ran through silvered corn. He and I, we have

the same skin tone, the same build, the same hands. We both press

the glass with my body. We

both wrack with spores. This time I toss him a sandwich bag full of

change. Next time in his bedroom or up at Split Rock on the flat,

warm rock beneath all those stars. One day she and I,

we'll lick Nutella off each other's fingers on the back porch. We'll

make out in the full light of day. If you can see it, don't cut it out.

THE WORD GIRLFRIEND

I have whole moments in the dramatic hallway. I scrape my body

over the edge of the lockers. Eyes pop off like buttons. They litter

the tile floor blinking.

The treasure I buried when I was only seven. The time we walked

so far into the woods it *like* wasn't the woods anymore. I make a

blind shape in the path of the hallway. A spot of static

where the girl shell buckles.

I scrape the eyes off and gaze is what's left. Released, it shimmers

the epic length of the hallway. Released, I make the alien body.

Their new shape in the hallway. The *like* terrifying geometry

I STILL SHOVE THINGS IN MY MOUTH FOR

IDENTIFICATION

The ocean receded. I watch the dolls propped up in the bedroom

staring. The ceiling slants down like closing a hand. Hard porcelain

faces and soft cloth bodies all waiting. There is some *like*

metaphor but I fail to see it. Josh is standing behind me in the

doorway. Their frills, their curls, their bonnets. That stare. There's

a tiny door in the bedroom. *Go ahead* he says. *I dare you,*

go in. The one about the murder-suicide, splinters under her nails. *If*

you lock me in, I'll kill you. Or the time she *like* fell on the point of

a cast iron fence. The time I cried and he put his hand down

my pants. No wonder our house is haunted. I watch my finger

touch her plastic eyelids. *One. Two.* What is a crush? Everyone

thinks we're lovers anyway. He shushes me. Anything is a toy

if you play with it.

Shhhhhhhhh

I GUESS I COULD KISS A GIRL. IF like YOU DARED ME

The ocean receded. I sit on the hood of my friend's '88 Plymouth

in my favorite flared jeans. I watch Becky kiss a girl. Insects cloud

the light over the garage like soot. The two girls sway

in the center of the circle, press each other back and forth with the

force of their tongues. The boys clap. The boys pump their fists.

I watch. I sit on my hands. Afraid of my face. Out of my face the

gaze juts. *Do I feel weird?* I click my heels three times. The gaze

comes out of her body right through my face. The gaze

leaves the husk of her body after *like* seventeen years. I click my

heels three times. It seems I'm already home. The dry husk clings

to white metal. On the gaze I split out the tight skin of her

body and *like* arms or legs poke through numerous. The curl of girl

shell rustles in the June breeze.

I GUESS I COULD KISS A GIRL. IF like YOU DARED ME

A kiss on the cheek. A peck. Soft brush like insect wings. The two

girls press each other back and forth with the force of their

tongues. It hurts. Right out the girl husk. Even their hair hurts

me. Something is ticking. It swings like a pendulum. This is worse

than before. After seventeen years in the blind loam of her body. It

comes out me, all ugly and droning. No, it's not *like* ugly,

only I am afraid. Its new body. *Tick tick.* Insects are not soft for

long.

THE CORN OR THE like STORY OF THE CORN

The phone is still ringing. The sun has gone blind. I grab the

receiver and hang up without answering. I can't tell you who's

home

I GUESS I COULD KISS A GIRL. IF like YOU DARED ME

My jaw clicks. Vision facets. Everything swarms. *They are more*
afraid of you than you are of them. I sing fierce without meaning.
It comes right out this body.

I must climb back into the girl husk and wrap the torn edges over
my coming. I must suck the gaze back in through *like* any girl hole
I find. *They are more afraid of you than you are*

of them.

The cloud of insects is gone. Still the light's full of shadows. I
click three times. The delicate brown bubbles where her eyes.
Where her mouth. *There's no place like home.* With one arm or

leg I stab a hole right through the paper-thin husk or the circle or
the boy standing next to me or the yellow old gaze. *Home home* I
drone. I stab a hole. That's *like* what a hole is.

I STILL SHOVE THINGS IN MY MOUTH FOR

IDENTIFICATION

Tonight I'm with Josh again in that farmhouse in Accord. White

lace curtains. Copper pots hung over the stove. An axe set against

the basement stairs. A place for *like* everything. It's too cold

to swim so we light a fire. He tells me the story of the house. The

noises won't stop. Shadows run the baseboards. I am reminded of a

woman creeping. He says he's been living here while their

daughter's away. *Dear daughter.* The dolls are not as quiet as

they seem. I won't go up there. He can't stay hard. *Go ahead* he

says. *I dare you.* I am afraid of the house but it's not what

you'd think. I think I am crawling. *Dear daughter, what's your* like

secret? I can make the blood seep back. Counter-clockwise like a

spool of red thread. I curl my hand softly but firm.

The basement door slams. The truth is, a woman is creeping.

Something is tipping. I have *like* so much love to give.

THE THREE OF US NAKED ON A PULL-OUT COUCH

One afternoon where the sun slants in thick and warm. I watch him

touch her. I arc. I make the center. They say not to drink from the

stream but that's just a story for tourists. I make *like* the center

and clamp down. In his little studio apartment, on the pullout

couch beneath the window. I want him in me. I want her breasts.

Just *like* say it. I want her breasts. Her pretty mouth snaps

in mine. His red hair humming. *Like* pounding. Through the skin,

the sun-hardened crust. I get arcing. I make the center among

sheets. Darkening sweat. I want her in me. I want his breasts.

The afternoon is golden. No one is drunk. Sunlight pours over us

into the center. It's also a hole. No one's drunk, but I'm hungry. I

have so much to learn. I stab an arm or a leg between

bodies. It comes back wet. So I am absorbent and clamping. Or I

am not afraid of dripping. The three of us rubbed soft at the edges.

Pulled free of the earth we cling together. Caught in the sap.

Turn the amber up to the light. Turn the amber to check for flaws.

The ocean receded. We sit on the lawn of our friend's house. I
watch her tell me. I'm like *It's not your fault.* She's like *You
should have seen his face when I said we should tell you.* I'm like
It's not your fault. Something starts ticking. *It's* like *not your fault.*
I feel it from the inside out. There is no way to turn it off now, it is
ticking and it will tick itself down. I'm like *It's not your fault.*
Meanwhile there's the one about her fingers in my hair. The one
about jumping High Falls, not clearing Low Falls. The story about
the football player and Sarah's party. The tripping fields. The one
about her prom date and me in his tent the night of graduation. A
fire in the woods. The phone call I bled her. She is my best friend.
She has set the clock or the bomb or the conveyor or the drinking
bird or whatever. Or *like* I have. *Do you* like *still love him?* We sit
on the lawn pulling up grass. Meanwhile there're chemicals in the
water—potassium chloride anhydrous ammonia dicamba atrazine
2, 4D.

SHE'S like MY BEST FRIEND

We crouch in the gravel throwing stones. *It's weird* she says *now I kinda feel like you're my girlfriend. When guys flirt with you, I feel jealous.* We watch the trees around us. *I'm not ready to be your girlfriend* I say. *Me either* she says.

Or

Once upon a time—nature. Once upon a time—sixteen. Hair untangling, gum peeling back to my lips. Once upon a time—they all point their fingers. Where I lifted her shirt with my teeth. Where our tongues met. What is right? What is *like* right?

Or

The sun has been setting for a long time today. She's *like* my best friend. We are happy in the dust sitting next to each other. That is

all.

Tick

Tick

Tick

AND THE TIME I MADE A FIGHT WITH HIM

The ocean receded. Simon says watch from the stoop. That girl on the street beating her boyfriend over and over with her purse. I watch from the stoop. Her big boots and long legs.

Whoa. Simon says

whoa. I make the skirt shape. It *like* comes right out my body. Right where his hands reach. I watch from the stoop and when my new arm or leg stabs out it's all soft and translucent,

the inner scrape of a shell. I curl against the glass box of the stoop. Her perfect arc and fall, her perfect swing. Like a dance. I am full up with creeping. I *like* something right out my skin.

Imagine a document like a map. Entering, going around, and leaving at the end. A leaving through your own holes. I shred my skirt shape without meaning. I make another.

We hear where his bones meet cement. She hits him over and over. I don't know this stroke. I make the skirt shape like a body. She slams him over and over. What defense mechanism.

Like what in her hands. Her sinew and muscle, the weight of her

stance. Home is a feeling. I spurt a little from the skirt shape.

Simon says feel for my hand.

THE WORD GIRLFRIEND

I watch the way she stands. I watch the way her body moves. Her
soft belly, long legs. Her jaw juts. In the fields in our beds. I am
not *like* what you'd call woman. Not when I'm near her.

Even in the moonlight. Shucked our clothes and ran through
silvered corn. I am not looking up. Next to her, I am a mass of
things creeping. A beautiful crawling. *Like* there in the grass

in the night of her poise. I *like* forget to be pretty. I put out feelers.
Next to her, I tear the skirt a little from the inside. She wants to
know if I'm angry she slept with my ex-boyfriend. I could *like*

never be angry with her.

AND THE TIME I MADE A FIGHT WITH HIM

The ocean receded. Simon says we could live here this summer.
Simons says the summer is fair. Something about Brautigan.
Something about hand-stitching and woodpeckers, poetry

in the folds of our bed. I hang up the phone and imagine. *Like* what
are we? In the lawn beside our little apartment, hands deep in
warm earth. The river runs north. Through all of it, my brown hair

just *like* sucks up the sun. Then all I see is a child. She's *like* right
in our sunlight. And now we're both wearing white. I wanted to
see just the two of us waking, his face right in mine. What

I see is the river run shallow, all murky with minnows. Some
inevitable spawn. I see we meet at the dress shape. Like a string of
paper dolls. My jaw clicks. Things repeat through my body.

That is the meaning of time. Someone moving in a circle. I rock
back on my heels. My legs or arms, all tangled with child.
Everything swarms. It was him and me and then *like* a child eats

everything. Our laughing child. Simon says a poem about

watermelon, small black globes nested in vine. I want him to crack

one open and pass me the flesh in his hand. Instead it just rolls

through my body. I try to touch where our home is. The feeling of

muslin and linen and silk. The shape has gone wild. Our garden is

lovely. Dinner is lovely. Where we touch at the phone line.

Sunlight is fading. The insects are chirring. I stab a hole. He

silhouettes to a dime. I am *like* so very capable. But I never wanted

a child. Scampering among the clover. I lower my jaws to feed.

RITE INTO MIRRORS

The ocean receded. I sit on the hood of my Honda Civic in a tank
top no bra. The sun comes down even and warm. Simon says
summer is fair. Still

he won't fuck me. His cock shoots white light. Then he has another
girlfriend with my name. *Fluck. Fluck a duck.* The metal is hot
under my thighs. She watches him

hug me. The asphalt bubbles black around a new seam. He turns
back. Turns away. I sit in the flat sunlight in my girl face and tits.
Like that kind of Jennifer. *Whew, that was awkward.* She watches

him take her hand. The she is me now. Not the tall Jennifer.
Jennifer in home sewn pants who knows how to scry. Jennifer
glides across the parking lot royally. My gaze sides down

a long ramp to the ground. *Are you okay?* my friend asks. Like *that
was awkward.* I am okay, or I'm something. Still the river runs
north. And in this shape I am bulging. Soft

beyond reason. Her thin arms and thin shoulders. Jennifer draws

lines. Where the two of them meet. I bulge into. I bulge out.

Bubbling black around a new seam. How will I mature into

Jennifer?

Tell me when it will begin to rain.

EFFACE

The ocean receded. Now it is almost the internet. I stare at the
screen while the phone rings. The cursor blinks green against
black. Once on the stoop, I asked her friend for a cigarette.

It was all

like part of my plan. Now I am waiting. The screen is too small to
climb into. I have all this strange body. All these *like* arms or legs.
I turn my heart with what's left of my tongue. It's too

earnest. Too indulgent. *A man a plan a canal.* He taught me
limitations of skin. But now I'm *like* alarming. That time I asked
for a sip of beer, he gave me dead cloud in a cup. Blue-marker

stars

duct tape stars. A paper bag passed in the drive-thru window. I
watch the screen. It makes *like* a hole. I will put in my extra. No
screaming. The world just got bigger. *A man a plan.* I know I'm

not *like* a goddess. I sit in the dark kitchen and press a new glass.

Outside there is ocean under this town. The world must eat to get

bigger. *A man a plan.* At the behest of the screen, I get flat.

All of this waiting. Someone walking in a circle. It's *like* what we

want. Part by part, I'm green blinking. The world's getting bigger.

Home home I drone. I am *like* luminous. I am *like* losing it.

There is no face

in the screen, just a greenish reflection. That is what a hole is.

Outside the tiger lilies ooze down their stalks into gravel. What

nature. Literally what. It does not fit.

HOW THERE'S NO like MEMORIAL PAGE

The ocean receded. I am sitting in a folding chair alongside a camper in Bethel. It rained all night and we haven't slept. We tried to sleep in a concrete pipe, but I couldn't. It's morning and I couldn't. I don't drink the Bacardi. I don't talk to the camper man. I don't talk to Jay who sits near me, quiet as bone. My best friend's boyfriend. I watch her dance with my boyfriend in the dawn. It's silver grey and the humid air is *like* full of it. I sit in the folding chair. The ground is wet. There is mud on my ankles. They are still dancing. Both tall and they spin with their arms out, heads back. No one else can fit. Not me, I cannot fit. I do not curl in or break off. I do not make a shape. A deep breath of silver. I see they will love each other. What gaze is left. I breathe silver. Airless. *Like* right through my skin. Everything is ready. Not me though. Not *like* me. Now what gaze uncoils straight from my gut. A spun silver chain. It is hooked to my insides. There are my insides. I spit my heart into my palm. The air tastes like trees. So indulgent. It is the second revelation. Turns out there's *like* really no ritual. I love them both. I hate them both. I take no shape. *A girl's body* the man says *tells her when she has become a woman.* Not me though, I'm *like* quicksilver. The mud, the shell, the air of my body. No matter what you all see.

Epilogue

GOOD HISTORICAL REASONS

The ocean receded. Mom and I are alone in the woods. The trail is longer than anyone thought. Still the sun comes down pearly dappled and the creek bed is mossy, the water is clear.

I wear a pair of my father's old running shorts. She carries the backpack, but I lead the way. A stand of birch trees. Broken beer bottles and a white plastic cutting board. Forget the hero quest.

Forget heroes. We tie our own knots. I scrutinize her work. I offer a hand. Like Grandma said *those Pollack knuckles*. I scrutinize my work. Where is the difference? A stand of birch trees

obscured by doubling flesh. Her skin flushed and damp. Here we are at the tower of *like* obvious allusion. No one is there to let down their hair. Broken beer bottles. Fingers slide in and out.

Passed down for *like* generations. Why are we both afraid to mark our own way? A tree falls but no one hears her. We share the last of the water. By the time we climb back to the gravel path, we are sweaty and hungry and mean. Three generations of women

alone. *I am no great beauty* she says. All of these gifts. Sometimes

in our blood and *like* sometimes in our hands.

PRIME DESTINATION

The ocean receded. I'm on the passenger side. Stuck behind some
out-of-towners. A field pulsing out the trees like opening a blouse.
With the window down I am sixteen. Oh

beautiful nature. She passes me a cigarette. I put my feet on the
dash. Hard vinyl, warm in the sun. The deer shift their ears in the
heat. Our hands touch. I am sixteen. *Like* what

a boring story.

Toes warm in the sun. We don't watch the deer. Her cherub
cheeks. My smug nose. She turns the music up. The molecules of
air between us *like* ricochet faster. There is some history. Like

once upon a time nature. The black widow is not aggressive. Bears
don't bother humans unless humans bother bears. She spits out the
window. I go to check my face in the mirror. Nature

slackens in the warm box. They have pointed their fingers. I flip
the visor down but the mirror's broke. Our hands touch. The
maples drop spinners. They all point their fingers. Stopped again

on the two-lane highway into the mountain. Our hands touch. What

was our body? Her watch, it starts beeping. I am *like* thirsty

forever. The doe raises her head. The yearling raises its head.

They all point their fingers. Oh nature, I am not wearing

underwear.

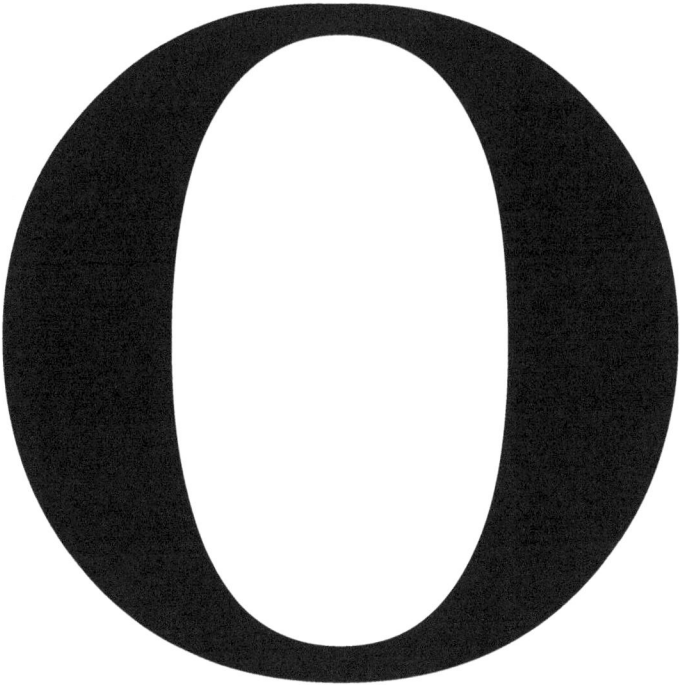

Acknowledgements:

Many thanks to the journals who have published some version of some of these poems:

alice blue review

Black Warrior Review

COAST / NO COAST

DREGINALD

interrupture

Juked

New Orleans Review

Ninth Letter

PANK

Pouch

rlysrslit

Sixth Finch

Spoon River Poetry Review

Winter Tangerine, Beyond the Breadcrumbs

www.ingramcontent.com/pod-product-compliance
Lightning Source LLC
Chambersburg PA
CBHW022104020426
42335CB00012B/825